FAVORITE BRAND NAME

# Deep Fryer
# COOKBOOK

**Publications International, Ltd.**
Favorite Brand Name Recipes at www.fbnr.com

Front cover photography by Sanders Studios, Inc.

**Pictured on the front cover:** Buttermilk Ranch Fried Chicken *(page 30)*.

**Pictured on the back cover** *(clockwise from top right):* The Ultimate Onion *(page 22),* Mexican Fritters *(page 86)* and Fish & Chips *(page 64)*.

ISBN: 0-7853-5182-5

Manufactured in China.

8 7 6 5 4 3 2 1

**Microwave Cooking:** Microwave ovens vary in wattage. Use the cooking times as guidelines and check for doneness before adding more time.

**Preparation/Cooking Times:** Preparation times are based on the approximate amount of time required to assemble the recipe before cooking, baking, chilling or serving. These times include preparation steps such as measuring, chopping and mixing. The fact that some preparations and cooking can be done simultaneously is taken into account. Preparation of optional ingredients and serving suggestions is not included.

# CONTENTS

# INTRODUCTION

## Fearless Frying

Lose the fear of frying and you'll find the flavor and texture you've been missing. By understanding a few simple rules you can create crunchy and crispy meals the whole family will enjoy.

## Makes and Models

There are several makes and models of deep fryers available to consumers today. Some come with removable baskets, while others are equipped with special slotted spoons to remove food. More expensive models come equipped with filter-lined covers that close as the food is cooking to eliminate odors and increase safety. Many models come with control knobs to adjust oil temperature. Before purchasing a fryer, do your research and choose one that fits your needs.

## Safety

As with all appliances, read the manufacture's directions before using a deep fryer. Since the temperature of the oil will reach 350°F or more, it is important to operate the deep fryer with extreme care.

• Give yourself plenty of room. Place the deep fryer on a countertop away from other appliances, utensils and food.

• Never leave hot oil unattended.

• Use oven mitts when removing the basket from the deep fryer or when spooning food from it.

• Do not overcrowd the deep fryer. The food will not cook properly and the chance for spills increases greatly.

• Let the deep fryer cool completely before emptying and storing it.

## It's All About the Oil

The secret to delicious deep-fried food is to cook it in oil that has been heated to the proper temperature. The ideal frying temperature is between 350° and 375°F.

If food is placed into the deep fryer before the oil has reached the correct temperature, the oil will penetrate the batter or breading and soak into the food. The end result will be soggy and greasy food.

**375° to 350°**

If the oil is too hot, it will begin to smoke. This is known as the smoking point—the point at which oil begins to decompose and impart unwanted flavors to the foods you are cooking.

Use canola oil or other vegetable oils. These oils have a higher smoke point than oils derived from animal fats.

Water and salt are the enemies of oil. When introduced to hot oil they cause it to break down faster and to splatter.

Shake off excess batter and breading before frying. These loose crumbs will quickly pollute the oil.

The longer the oil is heated, the quicker it will break down; therefore cook in batches as close together as possible and turn the fryer off immediately after cooking.

Strain the cooled oil after each use. Cover and store it properly. The cleaner the oil, the more uses you will get from it.

## Breading and Batter

Breading and batter serve a twofold purpose. First, they coat the food, protecting it from oil absorption. The second and equally important function is to add more flavor to the foods they are coating.

• The standard method for breading foods is usually a three-step process. First coat the food with flour, then dip it into beaten eggs, cream or a combination of both, and, finally, roll it into breadcrumbs. For more flavor, season both the flour and the crumbs with your favorite spices and herbs.

• Batters are semi-liquid mixtures that usually combine eggs, milk and flour. Beer and other liquids can be substituted for the milk. Leavening agents such as baking powder can be added if a lighter batter is desired.

Using the deep fryer safely, with clean oil and flavorful breading and batters, will add to your eating and cooking enjoyment.

# SIZZLING STARTERS

## Old-Fashioned Onion Rings

½ **cup buttermilk**
½ **cup prepared Ranch dressing**
 2 **large onions, sliced ½-inch thick and separated into rings**
    **WESSON® Vegetable or Canola Oil**
 2 **cups self-rising flour**
 2 **teaspoons garlic salt**
 2 **teaspoons lemon pepper**
½ **teaspoon cayenne pepper**
 2 **eggs, slightly beaten with 2 tablespoons water**

*Deep Fryer*

In a large bowl, combine buttermilk and Ranch dressing; blend well. Add onions and toss until well coated. Cover; refrigerate at least 1 hour or overnight. Fill a large deep-fry pot or electric skillet to no more than half its depth with Wesson® Oil. Heat oil between 325°F to 350°F. In a large bowl, combine flour, garlic salt, lemon pepper and cayenne pepper; blend well. Working in small batches, place onion rings in flour mixture; coat well. Dip into egg mixture. Return rings to flour mixture; coat well. Lightly shake off excess flour; fry until golden brown. Drain on paper towels. Sprinkle with additional garlic salt, if desired. ***Makes 4 servings***

### HOT HINTS

*When frying in batches, keep fried food warm by placing it in a single layer on a baking sheet lined with paper towels in a 250°F oven.*

**Old-Fashioned Onion Rings**

# Sausage Filled Wontons

**Deep Fryer**

1 pound BOB EVANS® Original Recipe Roll Sausage
¼ cup chopped onion
½ cup (2 ounces) shredded American cheese
3 ounces cream cheese
½ teaspoon dried marjoram leaves
¼ teaspoon dried tarragon leaves
30 square wonton wrappers
    Vegetable oil
    Dipping sauce, such as plum sauce or sweet and sour sauce
    (optional)

To prepare filling, crumble sausage into large skillet. Add onion. Cook over medium heat until sausage is browned, stirring occasionally. Remove from heat; drain off any drippings. Stir in next 4 ingredients. Mix until cheeses melt. Lightly dampen 1 wonton wrapper by dipping your finger in water and wiping all the edges, making ¼-inch border around square. (To keep wrappers from drying, cover remaining wrappers with damp kitchen towel while working.) Place rounded teaspoonful sausage mixture in the middle of wrapper. Fold wrapper over filling to form triangle, sealing edges and removing any air bubbles. Repeat with remaining wrappers and filling.

Heat 4 inches oil in deep fryer or heavy large saucepan to 350°F; fry wontons, a few at a time, until golden brown. Remove with slotted spoon; drain on paper towels. Reheat oil between batches. Serve hot with dipping sauce, if desired. Refrigerate leftovers. ***Makes 30 appetizers***

## HOT HINTS

*Wonton wrappers, or skins, are very thin squares of dough made from flour, eggs and water. The wrappers are sold as squares or circles in most large supermarkets. Look for them in either the*  *refrigerated section or the freezer case. Filled wontons are either fried, boiled or steamed.*

**Sausage Filled Wontons**

# Coconut Fish Bites

1 cup flaked coconut
½ cup unsalted peanuts
1 egg
1 tablespoon soy sauce
¼ teaspoon salt
⅓ cup cornstarch
1 pound firm white fish (haddock or cod fish), cut into 1-inch cubes
    Dipping Sauce (recipe follows)
1 quart vegetable oil for deep frying

1. Place coconut and peanuts in food processor. Process using on/off pulsing action until peanuts are ground, but not pasty.

2. Blend egg, soy sauce and salt in pie plate. Place cornstarch and coconut mixture on separate pieces of waxed paper.

3. Toss fish cubes in cornstarch until well coated. Add to egg mixture; toss until coated with egg mixture. Lightly coat with coconut mixture. Refrigerate until ready to cook. Prepare Dipping Sauce.

4. Heat oil in heavy 3-quart saucepan over medium heat until deep-fat thermometer registers 365°F. Fry fish, in batches, 4 to 5 minutes or until golden brown and fish cubes flake easily when tested with fork. Adjust heat to maintain temperature. (Allow oil to return to 365°F between batches.) Drain on paper towels. Serve with Dipping Sauce. Garnish, if desired.

*Makes about 24 appetizers*

## Dipping Sauce

1 can (8 ounces) sliced peaches, undrained
2 tablespoons packed brown sugar
2 tablespoons ketchup
1 tablespoon vinegar
1 tablespoon soy sauce
2 teaspoons cornstarch

Combine all ingredients in food processor. Process until peaches are chopped. Bring mixture to a boil in medium saucepan over medium heat; boil 1 minute or until thickened, stirring constantly. Sauce can be served warm or cold.

*Makes about 1¼ cups*

**Coconut Fish Bites**

# Spring Rolls

½ pound ground pork
1 teaspoon KIKKOMAN® Soy Sauce
1 teaspoon dry sherry
½ teaspoon garlic salt
2 tablespoons vegetable oil
3 cups fresh bean sprouts
½ cup sliced onion
1 tablespoon KIKKOMAN® Soy Sauce
1 tablespoon cornstarch
¾ cup water, divided
8 egg roll wrappers
½ cup quick biscuit mix
1 egg, beaten
Vegetable oil for frying
Hot mustard, tomato ketchup and KIKKOMAN® Soy Sauce

Combine pork, 1 teaspoon soy sauce, sherry and garlic salt; mix well. Let stand 15 minutes. Heat 2 tablespoons oil in hot wok or large skillet over medium-high heat; brown pork mixture in hot oil. Add bean sprouts, onion and 1 tablespoon soy sauce. Stir-fry until vegetables are tender-crisp; drain and cool. Dissolve cornstarch in ¼ cup water. Place about ⅓ cupful pork mixture on lower half of egg roll wrapper. Moisten left and right edges with cornstarch mixture. Fold bottom edge up just to cover filling. Fold left and right edges ½ inch over; roll jelly-roll fashion. Moisten top edge with cornstarch mixture and seal. Complete all rolls. Combine biscuit mix, egg and remaining ½ cup water in small bowl; dip each roll in batter. Heat oil for frying in wok or large saucepan over medium-high heat to 370°F. Deep-fry rolls, a few at a time, in hot oil 5 to 7 minutes, or until golden brown, turning often. Drain on paper towels. Slice each roll in half. Serve with mustard, ketchup and soy sauce as desired.

*Makes 8 appetizer servings*

**Spring Rolls**

# Crispy Wontons

½ **pound lean ground beef**
½ **pound ground pork**
½ **cup minced green onions**
 1 **tablespoon cornstarch**
 2 **tablespoons soy sauce**
 1 **package (1 ounce) HIDDEN VALLEY® Milk Recipe Original Ranch®**
    **salad dressing mix**
 6 **dozen square wonton skins**
 2 **egg whites, beaten**
    **Vegetable oil, for deep frying**
 2 **cups prepared HIDDEN VALLEY® Original Ranch® salad dressing**

In large bowl, combine beef, pork, onions, cornstarch, soy sauce and dry salad dressing mix; stir well. Place a small mound of mixture in center of each wonton skin. With your fingers, rub a bit of egg white on two top edges of wonton skin. Press skin together in half to form triangle, making sure skin is sealed on all sides. Place two long points of triangle on top of each other and seal with egg white.

In deep fryer or deep saucepan, heat ½ inch oil to 375°F. Fry wontons, a few at a time, until golden. Remove with slotted spoon and drain on paper towels. Serve warm with prepared salad dressing for dipping.

*Makes 6 dozen wontons*

---

## HOT HINTS

*Do not allow fat to smoke. Smoking is a sign that the fat is beginning to break down and this will affect its flavor.*

---

# Hawaiian Chicken Wings

½ **cup cornstarch**
¼ **cup all-purpose flour**
¼ **cup soy sauce**
¼ **cup sugar**
2 **eggs, lightly beaten**
2 **green onions, chopped**
2 **cloves garlic, crushed**
1 **tablespoon sesame seeds**
1½ **pounds chicken wings separated at joints, tips discarded**
   **CRISCO® Oil\***

*\*Use your favorite Crisco Oil product.*

Combine cornstarch, flour, soy sauce, sugar, eggs, green onions, garlic and sesame seeds in resealable plastic food storage bag or plastic bowl with tight-fitting lid. Mix thoroughly.

Rinse chicken; pat dry. Add to cornstarch mixture. Toss to coat. Marinate overnight.

Heat 2 inches oil to 365°F in deep fryer or in deep skillet. Fry chicken pieces, a few at a time, for 8 to 10 minutes or until golden brown and no longer pink in center, turning to brown evenly. Drain on paper towels.

***Makes 3 to 4 servings***

---

## HOT HINTS

*Sesame seeds are tiny, round and usually ivory colored, but brown, red and black sesame seeds are available. Sesame seeds have a slightly sweet, nutty flavor. They are widely available in grocery stores and are sold in bulk in specialty stores and ethnic markets. Because of their high oil content, they easily turn rancid and are best stored in the*  *refrigerator where they will keep up to six months or they may be frozen up to a year.*

# Batter-Fried Shark Bites

Pesto Mayonnaise (recipe follows)
1 pound shark steaks, about 1 inch thick
¾ cup all-purpose flour
½ teaspoon salt
¼ teaspoon baking powder
½ cup milk
1 egg, beaten
1 tablespoon butter or margarine, melted
Vegetable oil for frying

Prepare Pesto Mayonnaise. Remove skin from fish. Cut fish into 1-inch cubes. Place on paper towels; set aside.

Combine flour, salt and baking powder in shallow dish; make well in center. Add milk, egg and butter; beat until smooth. Heat 1 inch of oil in heavy deep skillet over medium heat to 365°F.

Dip 1 fish cube at a time into batter, coating all sides.

Place as many cubes as fit at a time into hot oil without crowding; fry until golden brown. Adjust heat to maintain temperature. (Allow temperature of oil to return to 365°F between each batch.)

Remove cubes from skillet and drain on paper towels. Serve immediately with Pesto Mayonnaise. *Makes 30 appetizers*

## Pesto Mayonnaise

½ cup mayonnaise
¼ cup prepared pesto sauce
1 tablespoon lemon juice
Grated lemon peel for garnish

Combine mayonnaise, pesto sauce and lemon juice in small bowl. Garnish, if desired. Refrigerate until ready to use. *Makes ¾ cup*

**Batter-Fried Shark Bites**

# Crispy Tortellini Bites

⅓ cup grated Parmesan cheese
1 teaspoon dried basil, crushed
½ teaspoon LAWRY'S® Seasoned Pepper
⅛ teaspoon cayenne pepper
1 package (8 or 9 ounces) cheese tortellini
⅓ cup vegetable oil
1 cup sour cream
¾ to 1 teaspoon LAWRY'S® Garlic Powder with Parsley

In medium bowl, combine cheese, basil, Seasoned Pepper and cayenne; set aside. Cook tortellini according to package directions, omitting salt. Run cold water over tortellini; drain. In large skillet, heat oil; add cooled tortellini and fry over medium high heat until golden-crisp; drain well. Toss cooked tortellini with cheese-spice mixture. In small bowl, blend sour cream and Garlic Powder with Parsley. Serve tortellini with sour cream mixture for dipping.

*Makes 6 servings*

**Serving Suggestion:** Serve with frill toothpicks or mini-skewers. Can also be served with prepared LAWRY'S® Extra Rich & Thick Spaghetti Sauce.

# Homemade Potato Chips

WESSON® Vegetable Oil
2 large russet potatoes, unpeeled
Salt

Fill a large deep-fry pot or electric skillet to no more than half its depth with Wesson® Oil. Heat oil to 350°F. Meanwhile, wash and scrub potatoes. Fill a large bowl with cold water three-fourths full. Slice potatoes crosswise into extremely thin pieces (about 1⁄16 inch); immerse slices in water. Working in small batches, remove potatoes with a slotted spoon; place on paper towels to dry. Fry 2 to 3 minutes or until golden brown and crispy. Remove from oil; drain on paper towels. Immediately salt to taste.

*Makes 4 to 6 servings*

**Tip:** For perfectly golden brown, crispy chips, make sure the oil temperature remains at 350°F.

# Ortega® Hot Poppers

**1 can (3.5 ounces) ORTEGA® Whole Jalapeños, drained**
**1 cup (4 ounces) shredded Cheddar cheese**
**1 package (3 ounces) cream cheese, softened**
**¼ cup chopped fresh cilantro**
**½ cup all-purpose flour**
**2 eggs, lightly beaten**
**2 cups cornflakes cereal, crushed**
**Vegetable oil**
**ORTEGA® Thick & Chunky Salsa, hot, medium or mild**
**Sour cream (optional)**

CUT jalapeños lengthwise into halves; remove seeds.

BLEND Cheddar cheese, cream cheese and cilantro in small bowl. Place 1 to 1½ teaspoons cheese mixture into each jalapeño half; chill for 15 minutes or until cheese is firm.

DIP each jalapeño in flour; shake off excess. Dip in eggs; coat with cornflake crumbs.

ADD oil to 1-inch depth in medium skillet; heat over high heat for 1 minute. Place jalapeños in oil; fry, turning frequently with tongs, until golden brown on all sides. Remove from skillet; place on paper towels. Serve with salsa and sour cream for dipping. ***Makes 8 servings***

## HOT HINTS

*Cilantro, a fresh green leafy herb, has a distinctive flavor and pungent aroma. It is similar in appearance to Italian (flat-leaf) parsley. Cilantro's flavor complements spicy foods, especially Mexican, Caribbean, Thai and Vietnamese dishes.*

# The Ultimate Onion

3½ cups all-purpose flour, divided
3 cups cornstarch
6 teaspoons paprika, divided
2 teaspoons garlic salt
1½ teaspoons black pepper, divided
1 teaspoon salt
2 bottles (24 ounces) beer
4 to 6 Colossal onions (4 inches in diameter)
2 teaspoons garlic powder
¾ teaspoon cayenne pepper, divided
Vegetable oil
1 pint mayonnaise
1 pint sour cream
½ cup chili sauce

**1.** Mix 1½ cups flour, cornstarch, 2 teaspoons paprika, garlic salt, 1 teaspoon black pepper and salt in large bowl. Add beer; mix well. Set aside.

**2.** Cut about ¾ inch off top of each onion; peel onions. Being careful not to cut through bottom, cut onions into 12 to 16 wedges.

**3.** Soak cut onions in ice water for 10 to 15 minutes. If onions do not "bloom" cut petals slightly deeper. Meanwhile, prepare seasoned flour mixture. Combine remaining 2 cups flour, 4 teaspoons paprika, garlic powder, remaining ½ teaspoon black pepper and ¼ teaspoon cayenne pepper in large bowl; mix well.

**4.** Dip cut onions into seasoned flour; remove excess by carefully shaking. Dip in batter; remove excess by carefully shaking. Separate "petals" to coat thoroughly with batter. (If batter begins to separate, mix thoroughly before using.)

**5.** Gently place onions, one at a time, in fryer basket and deep-fry at 375°F 1½ minutes. Turn onion over and fry 1 to 1½ minutes or until golden brown. Drain on paper towels. Place onion upright in shallow bowl and remove about 1 inch of "petals" from center of onion.

**6.** To prepare Creamy Chili Sauce, combine mayonnaise, sour cream, chili sauce and remaining ½ teaspoon cayenne pepper in large bowl; mix well. Serve warm onions with chili sauce. ***Makes about 24 servings***

*Favorite recipe from* **National Onion Association**

**The Ultimate Onion**

# Snappy Shrimp Zingers

**2 cups finely chopped cooked shelled shrimp**
**½ cup all-purpose flour**
**3 tablespoons finely chopped green onion**
**3 tablespoons finely chopped red bell pepper**
**1 tablespoon minced fresh parsley**
**1 tablespoon fresh lemon juice**
**2¼ teaspoons GEBHARDT® Hot Pepper Sauce**
**2 teaspoons Cajun seasoning**
**½ teaspoon salt**
**1 egg, slightly beaten**
**1 cup fine dry bread crumbs**
**2 cups WESSON® Canola Oil**

In medium bowl, combine *first 9* ingredients, ending with salt; blend well. Add egg and blend until thoroughly combined. (Mixture will be sticky.) Shape mixture into 12 (3×¾-inch) stick-shaped pieces. Gently roll *each* piece in bread crumbs. In a large skillet, heat oil to 325°F. Gently place shrimp sticks into oil and fry until crisp and golden brown. Drain on paper towels. Serve with your favorite dipping sauce or a squeeze of lemon.

***Makes about 12 zingers***

### HOT HINTS

 *The most accurate way to determine oil temperature is with a deep-fat thermometer.*

**Snappy Shrimp Zingers**

# Buffalo Chicken Wings

24 chicken wings
1 teaspoon salt
¼ teaspoon ground black pepper
4 cups vegetable oil for frying
¼ cup butter or margarine
¼ cup hot pepper sauce
1 teaspoon white wine vinegar
Celery sticks
1 bottle (8 ounces) blue cheese dressing

Cut tips off wings at first joint; discard tips. Cut remaining wings into two parts at the joint; sprinkle with salt and pepper. Heat oil in deep fryer or heavy saucepan to 375°F. Add half the wings; fry about 10 minutes or until golden brown and crisp, stirring occasionally. Remove with slotted spoon; drain on paper towels. Repeat with remaining wings.

Melt butter in small saucepan over medium heat; stir in pepper sauce and vinegar. Cook until thoroughly heated. Place wings on large platter. Pour sauce over wings. Serve warm with celery and dressing for dipping.

***Makes 24 appetizers***

*Favorite recipe from* **National Chicken Council**

## HOT HINTS

*Buffalo wings are deep-fried chicken wings served with a spicy hot sauce and blue cheese dressing. This dish originated at the Anchor Bar in Buffalo, New York, hence the name.*

# Mexican Egg Rolls

**2 cups (about 2 boneless, skinless breasts) finely shredded cooked chicken**
**2 cups (8 ounces) shredded Monterey Jack cheese**
**1¾ cups (16-ounce jar) ORTEGA® Garden Style Salsa, medium or mild, divided**
**¼ cup ORTEGA® Diced Green Chiles**
**10 to 12 egg roll wrappers**
**Vegetable oil**
**Sour cream (optional)**

COMBINE chicken, cheese, 1 cup salsa and chiles in large bowl. Scoop ⅓ cup filling down center of each egg roll wrapper. Fold one corner over filling; fold in 2 side corners. Moisten edges of remaining corner with water; roll up egg roll from bottom. Press to seal edges. Repeat with remaining filling and wrappers.

ADD oil to 1-inch depth in medium skillet; heat over high heat for 1 minute. Place egg rolls in oil; fry, turning frequently with tongs for 1 to 2 minutes, until golden brown. Remove from skillet; place on paper towels. Serve with remaining ¾ cup salsa and sour cream.          ***Makes 6 servings***

# OLD-FASHIONED CHICKEN

## Southern Fried Chicken

2½ to 3 pounds frying chicken pieces
   WESSON® Vegetable Oil
 2 cups self-rising flour
 2 teaspoons salt
 1 teaspoon pepper
 1 teaspoon paprika
 1 teaspoon onion powder
 ½ teaspoon ground sage
 ¼ teaspoon garlic powder
 2 eggs beaten with 2 tablespoons water

Rinse chicken and pat dry; set aside. Fill a large deep-fry pot or electric skillet to no more than half its depth with Wesson® Oil. Heat oil to 325°F to 350°F. In bag, combine flour and seasonings. Shake chicken, one piece at a time, in flour mixture until coated. Dip in egg mixture, then shake again in flour mixture until completely coated. Fry chicken, a few pieces at a time, skin side down, for 10 to 14 minutes. Turn and fry chicken 10 minutes, covered, then 3 to 5 minutes, uncovered, or until chicken is tender and juices run clear. Drain on paper towels. Let stand 7 minutes before serving.

***Makes 4 to 6 servings***

**Southern Fried Chicken**

# Buttermilk Ranch Fried Chicken

2½ to 3 pounds frying chicken pieces
   WESSON® Vegetable Oil
2¼ cups all-purpose flour
1¼ tablespoons dried dill weed
1½ teaspoons salt
 ¾ teaspoon pepper
2½ cups buttermilk

Rinse chicken and pat dry; set aside. Fill a large deep-fry pot or electric skillet to no more than half its depth with Wesson® Oil. Heat oil to 325°F to 350°F. In a medium bowl, combine flour, dill, salt and pepper. Fill another bowl with buttermilk. Place chicken, one piece at a time, in buttermilk; shake off excess liquid. Coat lightly in flour mixture; shake off excess flour. Dip once again in buttermilk and flour mixture. Fry chicken, a few pieces at a time, skin side down, for 10 to 14 minutes. Turn chicken and fry 12 to 15 minutes longer or until juices run clear; drain on paper towels. Let stand 7 minutes before serving. ***Makes 4 to 6 servings***

## HOT HINTS

*To reduce frying time by 7 to 9 minutes per side, simply cook unbreaded chicken in boiling*  *water for 15 minutes; remove and cool completely before proceeding with recipe.*

# Batter-Fried Chicken

1 (3-pound) broiler-fryer chicken, cut into serving pieces
1 cup water
1 rib celery (including leaves), cut into 2-inch pieces
1 small onion, cut into halves
1 clove garlic, cut into halves
½ teaspoon salt
⅛ teaspoon black pepper
Fritter Batter (recipe follows)
Vegetable oil

**1.** Place chicken, water, celery, onion, garlic, salt and pepper in 5-quart Dutch oven; heat to a boil. Reduce heat to low; cover and simmer 20 to 25 minutes or until chicken is barely pink in center.

**2.** Meanwhile, prepare Fritter Batter. Remove chicken from Dutch oven. Drain and pat dry with paper towels. Cool slightly.

**3.** Heat 2½ to 3 inches oil in deep fryer or 5-quart Dutch oven over medium-high heat until oil registers 350°F.

**4.** Dip chicken in Fritter Batter to coat. Add several chicken pieces to oil. (Do not crowd; pieces should not touch.) Fry, turning occasionally, 5 to 7 minutes or until chicken is golden and is no longer pink in center.

**5.** Place fried chicken on cookie sheet lined with paper towels; keep warm in 250°F oven until ready to serve. ***Makes 4 servings***

## Fritter Batter

1 cup all-purpose flour
1 teaspoon baking powder
1 teaspoon salt
¼ teaspoon white pepper
¾ cup milk
2 eggs, beaten
1 tablespoon vegetable oil

Combine flour, baking powder, salt and pepper in medium bowl; add milk, eggs and oil. Beat until well blended. ***Makes about 1½ cups***

# Basic Fried Chicken

½ **cup all-purpose flour**
 1 **tablespoon seasoned salt**
½ **teaspoon ground black pepper**
 1 **cut up chicken** *or* **4 boneless chicken breasts**
    **Vegetable oil for frying**

Combine flour, salt and pepper in gallon size plastic resealable food storage bag. Rinse chicken under cold running water; do not dry. Drop chicken, 2 to 3 pieces at a time, into flour mixture; shake to coat well. Heat ½ inch oil in large skillet over medium-high heat until hot. Place chicken, skin side down, in skillet. Turn pieces to brown evenly on all sides. Reduce heat to medium-low; cover and cook about 30 minutes or until fork can be inserted into chicken with ease and juices run clear, not pink. Drain on paper towels. Serve hot or cold. ***Makes 4 servings***

**Variations:** Add 1 teaspoon dry mustard and 1 teaspoon dried thyme, *or* 1 teaspoon curry powder, *or* ½ teaspoon lemon pepper and ½ teaspoon dried thyme to flour mixture. Continue as directed.

*Favorite recipe from* **National Chicken Council**

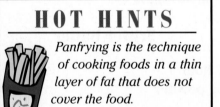

**HOT HINTS**

*Panfrying is the technique of cooking foods in a thin layer of fat that does not cover the food.*

**Basic Fried Chicken**

# Chicken Taquitos

12 (6-inch) corn tortillas
4 boneless, skinless chicken breasts (about
    1 pound), cooked and shredded
1 package (1.0 ounce) LAWRY'S® Spices & Seasonings
    for Tacos
½ cup hot water
½ cup minced green onions
¼ teaspoon LAWRY'S® Garlic Powder with Parsley
1 cup finely chopped tomatoes
  Vegetable oil for frying
  Shredded lettuce
  Guacamole
  Sliced red onion

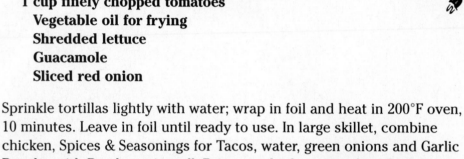

Sprinkle tortillas lightly with water; wrap in foil and heat in 200°F oven, 10 minutes. Leave in foil until ready to use. In large skillet, combine chicken, Spices & Seasonings for Tacos, water, green onions and Garlic Powder with Parsley; mix well. Bring to a boil over medium-high heat; reduce heat to low and cook 10 minutes. Stir in tomatoes. Place 2 tablespoons chicken mixture down center of each warmed tortilla. Roll up tortillas tightly; secure with toothpicks. In deep large saucepan, heat oil to 375°F. Fry rolled tortillas in oil until golden brown and crisp. Drain well on paper towels. Keep warm in oven; remove toothpicks before serving.

***Makes 6 servings***

**Serving Suggestion:** Serve on shredded lettuce. Garnish with guacamole and sliced red onion.

**Hint:** Lawry's Spices & Seasonings for Chicken Tacos may be substituted for Lawry's Spices & Seasonings for Tacos.

# Shoestring Potato Chicken Strips

    4 boneless, skinless chicken breast halves
¾ teaspoon salt, divided
    1 cup all-purpose flour
½ teaspoon garlic powder
½ teaspoon paprika
½ teaspoon pepper
    3 medium potatoes, peeled, coarsely grated and soaked in cold water
    1 cup cornstarch
    3 cups CRISCO® Oil*
    4 egg whites, lightly beaten

*Use your favorite Crisco Oil product.*

Rinse chicken; pat dry. Cut into 1-inch strips. Sprinkle with ½ teaspoon salt. Combine flour, garlic powder, paprika and pepper in resealable plastic food storage bag. Add chicken. Shake to coat.

Drain potatoes. Squeeze out remaining water. Sprinkle potatoes with remaining ¼ teaspoon salt. Add cornstarch. Toss to coat potatoes evenly.

Heat oil to 375°F in large deep skillet.

Dip chicken in egg whites. Dip chicken in potatoes, pressing to make potatoes stick to chicken. Fry half the strips at a time 7 to 8 minutes or until chicken is no longer pink in center. Drain on paper towels.

***Makes 4 servings***

# Twice-Fried Chicken Thighs with Plum Sauce

1 tablespoon ivory sesame seeds (optional)
½ cup Plum Sauce (recipe follows)
1 cup peanut oil
1 to 1¼ pounds boneless skinless chicken thighs, cut into strips
4 medium carrots, cut into julienne strips
4 green onions, sliced
½ teaspoon salt
½ teaspoon red pepper flakes
    Hot cooked rice

**1.** Heat wok over medium-high heat until hot. Add sesame seeds; cook and stir 45 seconds or until golden. Remove to small bowl, reserve.

**2.** Prepare Plum Sauce.

**3.** Heat oil in wok over high heat until oil registers 375°F on deep-fry thermometer. Drop chicken into oil; fry 1 minute. Remove with slotted spoon; drain on paper towels. Drain oil from wok, reserving 2 tablespoons.

**4.** Add 1 tablespoon reserved oil to wok. Heat over high heat. Add carrots; stir-fry 5 minutes until crisp-tender. Remove from wok; set aside.

**5.** Add remaining 1 tablespoon oil to wok. Add chicken and onions; stir-fry 1 minute. Stir in Plum Sauce, carrots, salt and red pepper. Cook and stir 2 minutes. Serve over rice; top with sesame seeds.       *Makes 4 servings*

## Plum Sauce

1 cup plum preserves
½ cup prepared chutney, chopped
2 cloves garlic, minced
2 tablespoons brown sugar
2 tablespoons lemon juice
2 teaspoons soy sauce
2 teaspoons minced fresh ginger

Combine all ingredients in small saucepan. Cook and stir over medium heat until preserves melt.       *Makes 1 cup*

**Twice-Fried Chicken Thighs with Plum Sauce**

# Pan-Fried Stuffed Chicken

⅓ cup diced sweet onion
2 tablespoons chopped fresh parsley
2 tablespoons grated Parmesan cheese
½ teaspoon salt
¼ teaspoon pepper
¼ teaspoon garlic powder
¼ teaspoon paprika
4 (1-ounce) slices Swiss cheese
4 boneless, skinless chicken breasts halves, pounded to ⅛-inch
   thickness
½ cup seasoned dry bread crumbs
2 tablespoons grated Parmesan cheese
⅓ cup all-purpose flour
2 eggs, lightly beaten
½ cup WESSON® Vegetable Oil

In a small bowl, combine *first* 7 ingredients, ending with paprika; mix well and set aside. Place 1 slice of cheese in center of *each* chicken breast. Top with ¼ onion mixture. Starting with long edge, tightly roll breast, folding in ends to seal. Secure with toothpicks. In a small bowl, combine bread crumbs and 2 tablespoons Parmesan cheese. Dredge *each* breast in flour. Dip *each* breast in eggs and then roll in bread crumbs. In a large skillet, heat Wesson® Oil over medium heat. Fry chicken, starting with seam side down, rotating every 7 to 10 minutes to avoid overbrowning. Fry 20 to 30 minutes or until golden brown and juices run clear. Drain on paper towels. ***Makes 4 servings***

**Tip:** Impress everyone even when you're busy. Chicken can be wrapped individually and frozen up to 2 months. Simply defrost and proceed with the recipe.

**Pan-Fried Stuffed Chicken**

# Chicken Mango

**4 boneless skinless, chicken breast halves**
**¾ teaspoon salt, divided**
**1 tablespoon lemon juice**
**¼ teaspoon pepper**
**2 eggs, well beaten**
**1½ cups fine dry bread crumbs**
**¼ cup CRISCO® Oil***
**1 large ripe mango, peeled and pitted**
**⅓ cup honey**
**Juice of 1 large lemon**
**3 tablespoons soy sauce**
**2 cloves garlic**

*Use your favorite Crisco Oil product.*

Rinse chicken; pat dry. Sprinkle with ¼ teaspoon salt. Place in bowl. Combine 1 tablespoon lemon juice, remaining ½ teaspoon salt and pepper. Pour over chicken. Toss to coat. Dip chicken in eggs, then crumbs.

Heat oil in large nonstick skillet on medium-high heat. Add chicken. Fry about 5 minutes per side or until golden brown and no longer pink in center. Drain on paper towels.

Place mango, honey, juice of 1 lemon, soy sauce and garlic in food processor. Process until blended, but not runny. Pour sauce into skillet. Bring to a boil on high heat. Reduce heat to low. Simmer 1 minute.

Cut chicken into strips. Dip in sauce.　　　　　　　　***Makes 4 servings***

# Parmesan Fried Chicken

1 egg
2 tablespoons water
⅔ cup fine, dry bread crumbs
⅓ cup grated Parmesan cheese
2 teaspoons LAWRY'S® Lemon Pepper
1 teaspoon LAWRY'S® Seasoned Salt
2½ to 3 pounds chicken pieces
¼ cup butter
2 tablespoons salad oil

In shallow dish, beat egg and water. In large plastic resealable food storage bag, combine bread crumbs, cheese, Lemon Pepper and Seasoned Salt; mix well. Dip chicken pieces in egg, then bread crumbs. In large skillet, melt butter and oil together. Add chicken pieces, a few at a time and cook over medium-high heat, removing pieces as they brown. When all are browned, return all chicken to skillet, cover and cook over low heat 25 to 30 minutes or until tender. Remove cover during last 5 minutes to crisp.

*Makes 4 to 6 servings*

# Hidden Valley Fried Chicken

1 broiler-fryer chicken, cut up (2 to 2½ pounds)
1 cup prepared HIDDEN VALLEY® Original Ranch® Salad Dressing
¾ cup all-purpose flour
1 teaspoon salt
½ teaspoon freshly ground black pepper
Vegetable oil

Place chicken pieces in shallow baking dish; pour salad dressing over chicken. Cover; refrigerate at least 8 hours. Remove chicken. Shake off excess marinade; discard marinade. Preheat oven to 350°F. On plate, mix flour, salt and pepper; roll chicken in seasoned flour. Heat ½ inch oil in large skillet until small cube of bread dropped into oil browns in 60 seconds or until oil is 375°F. Fry chicken until golden, 5 to 7 minutes on each side; transfer to baking pan. Bake until chicken is tender and juices run clear, about 30 minutes. Serve with corn muffins, if desired.

*Makes 4 main-dish servings*

# Braised Cornish Hens

2 Cornish hens, thawed if frozen (1½ to 1¾ pounds each)
¼ cup soy sauce
2 tablespoons dry sherry
1 teaspoon sugar
⅔ cup plus 1 tablespoon cornstarch, divided
¼ cup vegetable oil
1 piece fresh ginger (about 1 inch square), peeled and cut into 4 slices
2 cloves garlic, crushed
1 cup chicken broth
1 large yellow onion, coarsely chopped
12 ounces fresh snow peas, trimmed
Yellow squash, zucchini, carrot and red bell pepper crescents for garnish

**1.** Remove neck and giblets from hens; wrap and freeze for another use. Rinse hens and cavities under cold running water; pat dry with paper towels. Cut each hen into quarters, removing backbone and breast bone.

**2.** To prepare marinade, combine soy sauce, sherry and sugar in large bowl; mix well. Add hen quarters; stir to coat well. Cover and refrigerate 1 hour to marinate, stirring occasionally.

**3.** Drain hens and reserve marinade. Place ⅔ cup cornstarch in shallow dish or pie plate. Coat hens with cornstarch. Combine remaining 1 tablespoon cornstarch with marinade; mix well.

**4.** Heat wok over medium-high heat about 1 minute or until hot. Drizzle oil into wok and heat 30 seconds. Add ginger and garlic; cook and stir about 1 minute or until oil is fragrant. Remove and discard ginger and garlic with slotted spoon. Add hens to oil and fry about 10 to 15 minutes or until well browned on all sides, turning occasionally.

**5.** Add chicken broth and onion to wok; bring to a boil. Cover and reduce heat to low; simmer hens about 20 minutes or until fork-tender, turning occasionally. Move hens up side of wok and add snow peas to bottom of wok. Cover and cook 3 to 5 minutes or until peas are crisp-tender. Stir cornstarch mixture and add to wok. Cook and stir until sauce thickens and boils. Transfer to serving platter. Garnish, if desired. Serve immediately.

*Makes 2 to 4 servings*

**Braised Cornish Hen**

# Chicken Gigglers

 1 pound chicken breast tenders*
¾ teaspoon salt
½ teaspoon dried parsley flakes *or* 1½ teaspoons chopped fresh
    parsley
¼ teaspoon ground sage *or* ¾ teaspoon chopped fresh sage
¼ teaspoon ground thyme leaves *or* ¾ teaspoon chopped fresh thyme
 2 cups CRISCO® Oil**
 1 box (7½ to 8½ ounces) yellow corn muffin mix
 2 tablespoons finely chopped sweet onion
½ teaspoon dried basil leaves *or* 1½ teaspoons chopped fresh basil
⅔ cup milk
    Mildly spiced dipping sauce

*If chicken tenders are not available, purchase chicken breasts and cut into strips.
**Use your favorite Crisco Oil product.*

Rinse chicken; pat dry. Place in 8-inch square glass baking dish. Combine salt, parsley, sage and thyme. Sprinkle over chicken. Toss to coat.

Heat oil in deep skillet on medium heat.

Combine muffin mix, onion and basil in small bowl. Add milk. Stir until well blended. Coat chicken with batter. Drop pieces, 4 at a time, into hot oil. Fry for 2 minutes. Turn. Fry for 1 to 2 minutes or until no longer pink in center. Place on paper-towel lined plate. Keep warm until all chicken is fried. Serve warm with dipping sauce.           ***Makes 4 servings***

# Classic Fried Chicken

¾ **cup all-purpose flour**
1 **teaspoon salt**
¼ **teaspoon pepper**
1 **frying chicken (2½ to 3 pounds), cut up, or chicken pieces**
½ **cup CRISCO® Oil***

*Use your favorite Crisco Oil product.*

**1.** Combine flour, salt and pepper in paper or plastic bag. Add a few pieces of chicken at a time. Shake to coat.

**2.** Heat oil to 365°F in electric skillet or on medium-high heat in large heavy skillet. Fry chicken 30 to 40 minutes without lowering heat. Turn once for even browning. Drain on paper towels.          ***Makes 4 servings***

**Note:** For thicker crust, increase flour to 1½ cups. Shake damp chicken in seasoned flour. Place on waxed paper. Let stand for 5 to 20 minutes before frying.

**Spicy Fried Chicken:** Increase pepper to ½ teaspoon. Combine pepper with ½ teaspoon poultry seasoning, ½ teaspoon paprika, ½ teaspoon cayenne pepper and ¼ teaspoon dry mustard. Rub on chicken before step 1. Substitute 2¼ teaspoons garlic salt, ¼ teaspoon salt and ¼ teaspoon celery salt for 1 teaspoon salt. Combine with flour in step 1 and proceed as directed above.

## HOT HINTS

*The bulb of a deep-fat thermometer should be completely immersed in the oil, but do not let it rest on the bottom of the pan.*

# THE FISH FRY

## Fish with Hidden Valley Ranch®
## Tartar Sauce

  1 cup (½ pint) sour cream
¼ cup chopped sweet pickles
  1 package (1 ounce) HIDDEN VALLEY® Milk Recipe Original Ranch®
    salad dressing mix
¾ cup dry bread crumbs
1½ pounds white fish fillets (sole, flounder, snapper or turbot)
  1 egg, beaten
    Vegetable oil
    French fried shoestring potatoes (optional)
    Lemon wedges (optional)

To make sauce, in small bowl, combine sour cream, pickles and
2 tablespoons of the salad dressing mix; cover and refrigerate. On large
plate, combine bread crumbs and remaining salad dressing mix. Dip fillets
in egg, then coat with bread crumb mixture. Fry fillets in 3 tablespoons oil
until golden. (Add more oil to pan if necessary to prevent sticking.) Serve
with chilled sauce, French fries and lemon wedges, if desired.

*Makes 4 servings*

Fish with Hidden Valley Ranch®
Tartar Sauce

# Magic Fried Oysters

6 dozen medium to large shucked oysters in their liquor
   (about 3 pounds)
3 tablespoons CHEF PAUL PRUDHOMME'S Seafood
   Magic®, divided
1 cup all-purpose flour
1 cup corn flour
1 cup cornmeal
   Vegetable oil for deep-frying

Place oysters and oyster liquor in large bowl. Add 2 tablespoons of the
Seafood Magic to oysters, stirring well. In medium bowl, combine flour,
corn flour, cornmeal and the remaining 1 tablespoon Seafood Magic. Heat
2 inches or more of oil in deep-fryer or large saucepan to 375°F. Drain
oysters, then use a slotted spoon to toss them lightly and quickly in
seasoned flour mixture; shake off excess flour and carefully slip each oyster
into hot oil. Fry in single layer in batches just until crispy and golden
brown, 1 to 1½ minutes; do not overcook. (Adjust heat as needed to
maintain temperature at about 375°F.) Drain on paper towels. Serve on
French bread, if desired.                                    ***Makes 6 servings***

# Shrimp Miami

 2 pounds Florida shrimp, fresh or frozen
¼ cup olive or vegetable oil
 2 teaspoons salt
½ teaspoon white pepper
¼ cup extra dry vermouth
 2 tablespoons lemon juice

Thaw frozen shrimp. Peel shrimp, leaving last section of shell on. Remove
sand veins and wash. Preheat electric frying pan to 320°F. Add oil, salt,
pepper and shrimp. Cook 8 to 10 minutes or until shrimp are pink and
tender, stirring constantly. Increase temperature to 420°F. Add vermouth
and lemon juice. Cook 1 minute longer, stirring constantly. Drain. Serve hot
or cold as an appetizer or entrée.                          ***Makes 6 servings***

*Favorite recipe from* **Florida Department of Agriculture and Consumer Services, Bureau of
Seafood and Aquaculture**

**Magic Fried Oysters**

# Crab Cakes with Tomato Salsa

**CRAB CAKES**
   1 pound crabmeat
   1 tablespoon FILIPPO BERIO® Olive Oil
   1 onion, finely chopped
   1 cup fresh white bread crumbs, divided
   2 eggs, beaten, divided
   2 tablespoons drained capers, rinsed and chopped
   2 tablespoons mayonnaise
   1 tablespoon chopped parsley
   1 tablespoon ketchup
      Finely grated peel of half a lemon
   1 tablespoon lemon juice
      Additional FILIPPO BERIO® Olive Oil for frying
      Salt and freshly ground black pepper

**TOMATO SALSA**
   3 tablespoons FILIPPO BERIO® Olive Oil
   4 large tomatoes, finely chopped
   2 cloves garlic, crushed
   ¼ cup lemon juice
   4½ teaspoons sweet or hot chili sauce
   1 tablespoon sugar
      Salt and freshly ground black pepper

For Crab Cakes, pick out and discard any shell or cartilage from crabmeat. Place crabmeat in medium bowl; flake finely. In small skillet, heat 1 tablespoon olive oil over medium heat until hot. Add onion; cook and stir 3 to 5 minutes or until softened. Add to crabmeat. Gently mix in ½ cup bread crumbs, 1 egg, capers, mayonnaise, parsley, ketchup, lemon peel and lemon juice. Shape mixture into 8 round cakes; cover and refrigerate 30 minutes.

Meanwhile, for Tomato Salsa, in medium skillet, heat 3 tablespoons olive oil over medium heat until hot. Add tomatoes and garlic; cook and stir 5 minutes. Add lemon juice, chili sauce and sugar; mix well. Season to taste with salt and pepper.

*continued on page 52*

**Crab Cakes with Tomato Salsa**

*Crab Cakes with Tomato Salsa, continued*

Dip crab cakes into remaining beaten egg, then in remaining ½ cup bread crumbs. Press crumb coating firmly onto crab cakes.

In large nonstick skillet, pour in just enough olive oil to cover bottom. Heat over medium-high heat until hot. Add crab cakes; fry 5 to 8 minutes, turning frequently, until cooked through and golden brown. Drain on paper towels. Season to taste with salt and pepper. Serve hot with Tomato Salsa for dipping.                                          ***Makes 8 crab cakes***

# Crusty Hot Pan-Fried Fish

**1½ cups all-purpose flour**
**3½ teaspoons CHEF PAUL PRUDHOMME'S Seafood Magic®, divided**
  **1 large egg, beaten**
  **1 cup milk**
  **6 fish fillets (4 ounces each), speckled trout, drum or your favorite fish**
    **Vegetable oil for frying**

In flat pan, combine flour and 2 teaspoons of the Seafood Magic. In separate pan, combine egg and milk until well blended. Season fillets by sprinkling about ¼ teaspoon of the Seafood Magic on each. In large skillet, heat about ¼ inch oil over medium heat until hot. Meanwhile, coat each fillet with seasoned flour, shake off excess and coat well with milk mixture; just before frying, coat fillets once more with flour, shaking off excess. Fry fillets in hot oil until golden brown, 1 to 2 minutes per side. Drain on paper towels and serve immediately on heated serving plates.                 ***Makes 6 servings***

# Spicy Fried Potatoes & Seasoned Fried Fish

## SPICY FRIED POTATOES
    6 russet potatoes, washed and peeled
    1 (8-ounce) bottle crawfish and seafood boil liquid
        concentrate
 1½ tablespoons salt
    WESSON® Vegetable Oil

## SEASONED FRIED FISH
    2 pounds catfish fillets, cut into 1½- to 2-inch-wide strips
    Salt
 1½ (3-ounce) boxes seasoned fish fry dry mix
    WESSON® Vegetable Oil

## SPICY FRIED POTATOES

Thinly slice potatoes smaller than French fries. Place slices in a bowl of water to prevent browning. In another small bowl, pour ⅔ cup liquid concentrate, ½ cup warm water and salt; stir until salt is dissolved. Drain water from potatoes; place potatoes in seasoned water and toss to coat. Cover and refrigerate potatoes for 2 hours, stirring occasionally. Drain in colander for 20 minutes before frying. Meanwhile, fill 2 deep-fry pots or electric skillets to half their depth with Wesson® Oil. Heat oil to 350°F.

## SEASONED FRIED FISH

Rinse fish and pat dry; sprinkle with salt. Dredge fish on both sides with seasoned fry mix; coat well.

## FRYING

In one deep-fry pot, fry fish, a few pieces at a time, until golden brown and crisp (about 2 to 3 minutes). In other deep-fry pot, fry potatoes, in small batches, until golden brown and crisp. Remove fish and potatoes from oil and drain on paper towels. Salt to taste; serve hot.

*Makes 8 to 10 servings*

**Tip:** For finicky family members who don't like fish, substitute chicken tenders for the catfish.

# Blazing Catfish Po' Boys

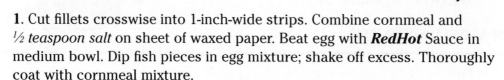

1½ **pounds catfish fillets**
¾ **cup yellow cornmeal**
1 **egg**
⅓ **cup *Frank's® RedHot® Sauce***
6 **sandwich rolls, split in half**
   **Spicy Tartar Sauce (recipe follows)**
3 **cups deli coleslaw**

**1**. Cut fillets crosswise into 1-inch-wide strips. Combine cornmeal and *½ teaspoon salt* on sheet of waxed paper. Beat egg with ***RedHot*** Sauce in medium bowl. Dip fish pieces in egg mixture; shake off excess. Thoroughly coat with cornmeal mixture.

**2**. Heat *1½ cups vegetable oil* in large deep skillet or electric fryer until hot (360°F). Cook fish, in batches, 5 minutes or until cooked through and golden on all sides, turning once. Drain on paper towels.

**3**. Hollow out rolls if necessary. Spread bottom of each roll with about *2 tablespoons* Spicy Tartar Sauce. Layer with *½ cup* coleslaw and a few pieces of fish. Cover with top of roll.          ***Makes 6 sandwiches***

**Spicy Tartar Sauce:** Combine ⅔ cup prepared tartar sauce with ¼ cup ***Frank's RedHot*** Sauce.

**Prep Time:** 15 minutes
**Cook Time:** 5 minutes

**Blazing Catfish Po' Boy**

# Fried Calamari with Tartar Sauce

1 pound fresh or thawed frozen squid
1 egg
1 tablespoon milk
¾ cup fine dry unseasoned bread crumbs
   Vegetable oil
   Tartar Sauce (recipe page 58)
   Lemon wedges (optional)

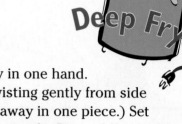

**1**. To clean each squid, hold body of squid firmly in one hand. Grasp head firmly with other hand; pull head, twisting gently from side to side. (Head and contents of body should pull away in one piece.) Set aside tubular body sac. Cut tentacles off head; set aside. Discard head and contents of body.

**2**. Grasp tip of pointed, thin, clear cartilage protruding from body; pull out and discard. Rinse squid under cold running water. Peel off and discard spotted outer membrane covering body sac and fins. Pull off side fins; set aside. Rinse inside of squid body thoroughly under running water. Repeat with remaining squid.

**3**. Cut each squid body crosswise into ¼-inch rings. Cut reserved fins into thin slices. (Body rings, fins and reserved tentacles are all edible parts.) Pat pieces thoroughly dry with paper towels.

**4**. Beat egg with milk in small bowl. Add squid pieces; stir to coat well. Spread bread crumbs on plate. Dip squid pieces in bread crumbs; place in shallow bowl or on waxed paper. Let stand 10 to 15 minutes before frying.

**5**. To deep fry squid, heat 1½ inches oil in large saucepan to 350°F. (Caution: Squid will pop and spatter during frying; do not stand too close to pan.) Adjust heat to maintain temperature. Fry 8 to 10 pieces of squid at a time in hot oil 45 to 60 seconds until light brown. Remove with slotted spoon; drain on paper towels. Repeat with remaining squid pieces.

**6**. Serve hot with Tartar Sauce and lemon wedges. Garnish as desired.

*Makes 2 to 3 servings*

*continued on page 58*

**Fried Calamari with Tartar Sauce**

*Fried Calamari with Tartar Sauce, continued*

### Tartar Sauce

   1 green onion
   1 tablespoon drained capers
   1 small sweet gherkin or pickle
   2 tablespoons chopped fresh parsley
1⅓ cups mayonnaise

**1.** Thinly slice green onion. Mince capers and gherkin.

**2.** Fold green onion, capers, gherkin and parsley into mayonnaise. Cover and refrigerate until ready to serve.   *Makes about 1⅓ cups*

# Fried Orange Shrimp

   1 cup all-purpose flour
   1 cup Florida orange juice
   1 Florida egg, beaten
   ½ teaspoon salt
      Oil for deep frying
1½ pounds raw Florida shrimp, peeled and deveined

Combine flour, orange juice, egg and salt; mix well. Heat oil in large skillet to 350°F. Dip shrimp into batter to coat, then place in oil to fry. Cook shrimp about 1 minute or until golden brown. Remove from oil and drain on paper towels.   *Makes 6 servings*

*Favorite recipe from* **Florida Department of Agriculture and Consumer Services, Bureau of Seafood and Aquaculture**

# Deviled Shrimp

Devil Sauce (recipe follows)
2 eggs, lightly beaten
¼ teaspoon salt
¼ teaspoon TABASCO® brand Pepper Sauce
1 quart vegetable oil
1 pound raw shrimp, peeled and cleaned
1 cup dry bread crumbs

Prepare Devil Sauce; set aside. Stir together eggs, salt and TABASCO® Sauce in shallow dish until well blended. Pour oil into heavy 3-quart saucepan or deep-fat fryer, filling no more than ⅓ full. Heat oil over medium heat to 375°F. Dip shrimp into egg mixture, then into bread crumbs; shake off excess. Carefully add shrimp to oil, a few at a time. Cook 1 to 2 minutes or until golden. Drain on paper towels. Just before serving, drizzle Devil Sauce over shrimp.

***Makes 6 appetizer servings***

## Devil Sauce

2 tablespoons butter *or* margarine
1 small onion, finely chopped
1 clove garlic, minced
1½ teaspoons dry mustard
½ cup beef consommé
2 tablespoons Worcestershire sauce
2 tablespoons dry white wine
¼ teaspoon TABASCO® brand Pepper Sauce
¼ cup lemon juice

Melt butter in 1-quart saucepan over medium heat; add onion and garlic. Stirring frequently, cook 3 minutes or until tender. Blend in mustard. Gradually stir in consommé, Worcestershire sauce, wine and TABASCO® Sauce until well blended. Bring to a boil and simmer 5 minutes. Stir in lemon juice. Serve warm over shrimp or use as a dip.

***Makes about 1¼ cups***

# Southern Fried Catfish with Hush Puppies

Hush Puppy Batter (recipe follows)
4 catfish fillets (about 1½ pounds)
½ cup yellow cornmeal
3 tablespoons all-purpose flour
1½ teaspoons salt
¼ teaspoon ground red pepper
Vegetable oil for frying
Fresh parsley sprigs for garnish

Prepare Hush Puppy Batter; set aside.

Rinse catfish and pat dry with paper towels. Combine cornmeal, flour, salt and red pepper in shallow dish. Dip fish in cornmeal mixture. Heat 1 inch of oil in large, heavy saucepan over medium heat until oil registers 375°F on deep-fry thermometer.

Fry fish, a few pieces at a time, 4 to 5 minutes or until golden brown and fish flakes easily when tested with fork. Adjust heat to maintain temperature. (Allow temperature of oil to return to 375°F between each batch.) Drain fish on paper towels.

To make Hush Puppies, drop batter by tablespoonfuls into hot oil. Fry, a few pieces at a time, 2 minutes or until golden brown. Garnish, if desired.

***Makes 4 servings***

## Hush Puppy Batter

1½ cups yellow cornmeal
½ cup all-purpose flour
2 teaspoons baking powder
½ teaspoon salt
1 cup milk
1 small onion, minced
1 egg, slightly beaten

Combine cornmeal, flour, baking powder and salt in medium bowl. Add milk, onion and egg. Stir until well combined. Allow batter to stand 5 to 10 minutes before frying.

***Makes about 24 hush puppies***

**Southern Fried Catfish with Hush Puppies**

# Oyster Poor Boys

Spicy Mayonnaise (recipe follows)
¾ cup cornmeal
¼ cup all-purpose flour
½ teaspoon salt
⅛ teaspoon black pepper
¾ cup oil for frying
2 pints shucked oysters, drained
4 French bread rolls*, split
Lettuce leaves
Tomato slices

*Substitute French bread loaf, split and cut into 4-inch lengths, for French bread rolls.

1. Prepare Spicy Mayonnaise; cover. Set aside.

2. Combine cornmeal, flour, salt and pepper in shallow bowl; set aside.

3. Heat oil in medium skillet over medium heat. Pat oysters dry with paper towels. Dip oysters in cornmeal mixture to coat.

4. Fry in batches 5 minutes or until golden brown, turning once. Drain on paper towels.

5. Spread rolls with Spicy Mayonnaise; fill with lettuce, tomatoes and oysters.

*Makes 4 sandwiches*

## Spicy Mayonnaise

½ cup mayonnaise
2 tablespoons plain yogurt
¼ teaspoon ground red pepper
1 clove garlic, minced

Combine all ingredients; mix until well blended.

*Makes ½ cup*

Oyster Poor Boy

# Fish & Chips

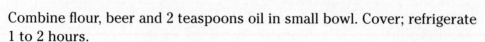

¾ **cup all-purpose flour**
½ **cup flat beer or lemon-lime carbonated beverage**
   **Vegetable oil**
 4 **medium russet potatoes, each cut into 8 wedges**
   **Salt**
 1 **egg, separated**
 1 **pound cod fillets**
   **Malt vinegar (optional)**

Combine flour, beer and 2 teaspoons oil in small bowl. Cover; refrigerate 1 to 2 hours.

Pour 2 inches of oil into heavy skillet. Heat oil over medium heat until a fresh bread cube placed in oil browns in 1 minute (about 365°F). Add as many potato wedges as will fit without crowding. Fry potato wedges 4 to 6 minutes or until outsides are brown, turning once. Drain on paper towels; sprinkle lightly with salt. Repeat with remaining potato wedges. (Allow temperature of oil to return to 365°F between frying each batch.) Reserve oil to fry cod.

Stir egg yolk into flour mixture. Beat egg white with electric mixer at high speed in bowl until soft peaks form. Fold egg white into flour mixture; set aside. Rinse fish and pat dry with paper towels. Cut fish into 8 pieces. Dip 4 fish pieces into batter; fry 4 to 6 minutes or until batter is crispy and brown and fish flakes easily when tested with fork, turning once. Drain on paper towels. Repeat with remaining fish pieces. (Allow temperature of oil to return to 365°F between frying each batch.) Serve immediately with potato wedges. Sprinkle fish with malt vinegar, if desired. Garnish as desired.

***Makes 4 servings***

**Fish & Chips**

# LIP-SMACKING SIDES

## Hot Hush Puppies

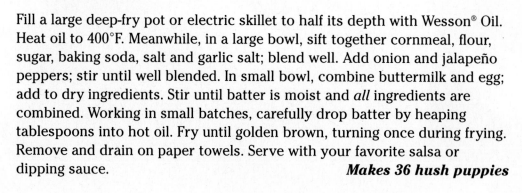

Deep Fryer

   WESSON® Vegetable Oil
1¾ cups cornmeal
 ½ cup all-purpose flour
 1 teaspoon sugar
 ¾ teaspoon baking soda
 ½ teaspoon salt
 ½ teaspoon garlic salt
 ½ cup diced onion
 ½ to 1 (4-ounce) can diced jalapeño peppers
 1 cup buttermilk
 1 egg, beaten

Fill a large deep-fry pot or electric skillet to half its depth with Wesson® Oil.
Heat oil to 400°F. Meanwhile, in a large bowl, sift together cornmeal, flour,
sugar, baking soda, salt and garlic salt; blend well. Add onion and jalapeño
peppers; stir until well blended. In small bowl, combine buttermilk and egg;
add to dry ingredients. Stir until batter is moist and *all* ingredients are
combined. Working in small batches, carefully drop batter by heaping
tablespoons into hot oil. Fry until golden brown, turning once during frying.
Remove and drain on paper towels. Serve with your favorite salsa or
dipping sauce.
                                                    ***Makes 36 hush puppies***

Hot Hush Puppies

# Dry-Cooked Green Beans

4 ounces lean ground pork or turkey
2 tablespoons plus 1 teaspoon light soy sauce,
    divided
2 tablespoons plus 1 teaspoon rice wine or dry
    sherry, divided
½ teaspoon Asian sesame oil
2 tablespoons water
1 teaspoon sugar
3 cups vegetable oil
1 pound fresh green beans, trimmed and cut into 2-inch lengths
1 tablespoon sliced green onion (white part only)
    Carrot flowers for garnish

**1**. Combine pork, 1 teaspoon soy sauce, 1 teaspoon rice wine and sesame oil in medium bowl; mix well. Set aside.

**2**. Combine water, sugar, remaining 2 tablespoons soy sauce and 2 tablespoons rice wine in small bowl; mix well. Set aside.

**3**. Heat vegetable oil in wok over medium-high heat until oil registers 375°F on deep-fry thermometer. Carefully add ½ of beans and fry 2 to 3 minutes or until beans blister and are crisp-tender. Remove beans with slotted spoon to paper towels; drain. Reheat oil and repeat with remaining beans.

**4**. Pour off oil; heat wok over medium-high heat 30 seconds. Add pork mixture and stir-fry about 2 minutes or until well browned. Add beans and soy sauce mixture; toss until heated through. Transfer to serving dish. Sprinkle with green onion. Garnish, if desired. Serve immediately.

*Makes 4 servings*

## HOT HINTS

*Asian sesame oil is an amber-colored oil pressed from toasted sesame seeds. It has a strong, nutty flavor that when used*

*sparingly adds a unique flavor to foods, such as stir-fries, Asian noodles and fish dishes.*

**Dry-Cooked Green Beans**

# Sweet Potato Wedges

**2 cups corn oil**
**3 large sweet potatoes, cleaned and cut into 8 wedges each**
**1 tablespoon LAWRY'S® Seasoned Salt**
**½ pound fresh green beans, trimmed and steamed (optional)**

In large deep skillet or electric skillet, heat oil to 365°F. Add sweet potato wedges a few wedges at a time and fry sweet potato wedges about 5 minutes or until slightly crisp outside. Drain on paper towels. Sprinkle Seasoned Salt generously over cooked wedges. Mix carefully in bowl with green beans for extra color. ***Makes 4 servings***

**Serving Suggestion:** Serve in paper napkin-lined basket.

# Rice Medallions

**3 cups cooked brown rice**
**2 carrots, shredded**
**1 red bell pepper, shredded**
**1 leek, thinly sliced or 4 green onions, sliced**
**1 medium zucchini, shredded**
**4 eggs, slightly beaten**
**1 clove garlic, minced**
**½ teaspoon salt**
**¼ teaspoon ground white pepper**
**Vegetable oil for frying**

Combine rice, carrots, pepper, leek, zucchini, eggs, garlic, salt and white pepper in large bowl; mix thoroughly. Heat ¼ inch oil in large skillet until hot. Spoon ¼ cup rice mixture into skillet; flatten with spatula to make patty. Fry 3 to 5 minutes on each side or until golden brown. Repeat with remaining rice mixture. Serve immediately. ***Makes 6 servings (3 patties each)***

# Fried Green Tomatoes

½ **pound sliced bacon**
1 **cup cornmeal**
1 **cup all-purpose flour**
2 **teaspoons salt**
½ **teaspoon black pepper**
½ **teaspoon cayenne pepper**
3 **eggs, slightly beaten**
2 **cups WESSON® Corn Oil**
6 to 8 **green tomatoes, sliced ¼ to ½ inch thick**

In a large skillet, fry bacon until crisp; drain on paper towels. Crumble bacon; set aside. Reserve bacon drippings in the skillet. In a medium bowl, combine cornmeal, flour, salt and peppers; mix well. In a small bowl, combine eggs and *half* the crumbled bacon; mix well. Heat Wesson® Oil over medium heat in same skillet with bacon drippings. Sprinkle tomatoes lightly with salt; dip in egg mixture, making sure to press bacon pieces onto tomatoes. Place tomatoes in cornmeal mixture; gently press mixture onto both sides of tomatoes. Fry until light golden brown, turning once. Drain on paper towels. Sprinkle with *remaining* bacon and serve.

***Makes 20 to 25 fried tomatoes***

## HOT HINTS

*Green tomatoes are unripened. Firm and tart, they are excellent for pickling and frying.*

# Classic Polenta

**6 cups water**
**2 teaspoons salt**
**2 cups yellow cornmeal**
**¼ cup vegetable oil**

**1.** Bring water and salt to a boil in large, heavy saucepan over medium-high heat. Stirring water vigorously, add cornmeal in very thin but steady stream (do not let lumps form). Reduce heat to low.

**2.** Cook polenta, uncovered, 40 to 60 minutes until very thick, stirring frequently. Polenta is ready when spoon will stand upright by itself in center of mixture. Polenta can be served at this point.*

**3.** For fried polenta, spray 11×7-inch baking pan with nonstick cooking spray. Spread polenta mixture evenly into baking pan. Cover and let stand at room temperature at least 6 hours or until completely cooled and firm.

**4.** Unmold polenta onto cutting board. Cut polenta crosswise into 1¼-inch-wide strips. Cut strips into 2- to 3-inch-long pieces.

**5.** Heat oil in large, heavy skillet over medium-high heat; reduce heat to medium. Fry polenta pieces, ½ at a time, 4 to 5 minutes until golden on all sides, turning as needed. Garnish as desired.     ***Makes 6 to 8 servings***

*Polenta is an important component of Northern Italian cooking. The basic preparation presented here can be served in two forms. Hot freshly made polenta, prepared through step 2, can be mixed with ⅓ cup butter and ⅓ cup grated Parmesan cheese and served as a first course. Or, pour onto a large platter and top with other hearty meat sauces for a main dish. Fried polenta, as prepared here, is appropriate as an appetizer or as a side dish with meat.*

**Classic Polenta**

# Ortega® Chile Relleños

1 can (7 ounces) ORTEGA® Whole Green Chiles
8 ounces Monterey Jack cheese, cut into 2-inch strips
3 eggs, separated
3 tablespoons all-purpose flour
   Vegetable oil
   ORTEGA® Thick & Chunky Salsa, mild, warmed

STUFF each chile (being careful not to break skins) with 1 strip cheese.

BEAT egg whites in medium bowl until stiff peaks form. Whisk egg yolks until creamy in small bowl. Fold yolks and flour into egg whites until just combined.

ADD oil to 1-inch depth in medium skillet; heat over high heat for 1 minute. Dip chiles in egg mixture until well coated. Place in oil; fry, turning frequently with tongs, until golden brown. Remove from skillet; place on paper towels. Serve with salsa.                    ***Makes 5 servings***

**Tip:** Add some flavor to the batter with cayenne pepper, ground cumin or oregano. Stuff the chiles with a variety of mild cheeses and serve with ORTEGA® Salsa.

HOT HINTS

*Adding beaten egg whites to a batter for fried foods produces a lighter, more delicate coating.*

# Vala's Finest Corn Fritters

WESSON® Vegetable Oil
2 eggs, beaten
½ cup milk
1 (7-ounce) can whole kernel corn, drained
2 cups self-rising flour
Sifted powdered sugar

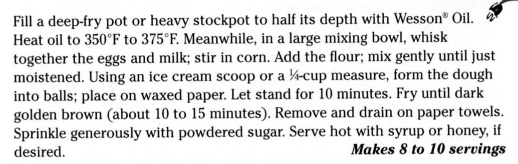

Fill a deep-fry pot or heavy stockpot to half its depth with Wesson® Oil. Heat oil to 350°F to 375°F. Meanwhile, in a large mixing bowl, whisk together the eggs and milk; stir in corn. Add the flour; mix gently until just moistened. Using an ice cream scoop or a ¼-cup measure, form the dough into balls; place on waxed paper. Let stand for 10 minutes. Fry until dark golden brown (about 10 to 15 minutes). Remove and drain on paper towels. Sprinkle generously with powdered sugar. Serve hot with syrup or honey, if desired.                                    ***Makes 8 to 10 servings***

# Fried Pickle Spears

3 tablespoons all-purpose flour
1 teaspoon cornstarch
3 eggs
1 cup cornflake crumbs
12 pickle spears, patted dry
½ cup corn oil
Yellow mustard (optional)

Line serving dish with paper towels; set aside. Combine flour and cornstarch in small bowl; set aside. Beat eggs in a small bowl; set aside. Place cornflake crumbs in another small bowl; set aside.

Coat pickle spears in flour mixture, shaking off excess flour. Dip pickle in egg; roll in cornflake crumbs. Repeat with remaining pickles.

Heat oil in large nonstick skillet over medium heat. Cook four pickles at a time, 1 to 2 minutes on each side or until golden brown. Remove to prepared serving dish. Repeat with remaining pickles. Serve with mustard, if desired.                                    ***Makes 12 servings***

# Scallion Pancakes

2¼ **cups all-purpose flour, divided**
1 **teaspoon sugar**
⅔ **cup boiling water**
¼ **to** ½ **cup cold water**
2 **teaspoons sesame oil**
1 **teaspoon coarse salt**
½ **cup finely chopped green onion tops**
½ **to** ¾ **cup vegetable oil**

**1.** Combine 2 cups flour and sugar in large bowl. Stir in boiling water and mix with chopsticks or fork just until water is absorbed and mixture forms large clumps. Gradually stir in enough cold water so dough forms a ball and is no longer sticky.

**2.** Place dough on lightly floured surface; flatten slightly. Knead dough 5 minutes or until smooth and elastic. Wrap dough with plastic wrap; let stand 1 hour.

**3.** Unwrap dough and knead briefly on lightly floured surface; divide dough into 4 pieces. Roll 1 dough piece into 6- to 7-inch round, keeping remaining dough pieces wrapped in plastic wrap to prevent drying. Brush dough with ½ teaspoon sesame oil; evenly sprinkle with ¼ teaspoon salt and 2 tablespoons green onions. Roll up, jelly-roll fashion, into tight cylinder.

**4.** Coil cylinder into a spiral and pinch end under into dough. Repeat with remaining dough pieces, sesame oil, salt and green onions. Cover coiled pieces with plastic wrap and let stand 15 minutes.

**5.** Roll each coiled piece on lightly floured surface into 6- to 7-inch round with floured rolling pin.

**6.** Heat ½ cup vegetable oil in wok over medium-high heat until oil registers 375°F on deep-fry thermometer. Carefully place 1 pancake into hot oil. Fry 2 to 3 minutes per side or until golden. While pancake is frying, press center lightly with metal spatula to ensure even cooking. Remove to paper towels; drain. Repeat with remaining pancakes, adding more oil if necessary and reheating oil between batches.

**7.** Cut each pancake into 8 wedges. Arrange on serving platter. Serve immediately.

*Makes 32 appetizers*

**Scallion Pancakes**

# BEST OF THE REST

## Spanish Churros

    1 cup water
    ¼ cup butter
    6 tablespoons sugar, divided
    ¼ teaspoon salt
    1 cup all-purpose flour
    2 large eggs
      Vegetable oil for frying
    1 teaspoon ground cinnamon

Place water, butter, 2 tablespoons sugar and salt in medium saucepan; bring to a boil over high heat. Remove from heat; add flour. Beat with spoon until dough forms ball and releases from side of pan. Vigorously beat in eggs, 1 at a time, until mixture is smooth. Spoon dough into pastry bag fitted with large star tip. Pipe 3×1-inch strips onto waxed-paper-lined baking sheet. Place baking sheet in freezer; freeze 20 minutes.

Pour vegetable oil into 10-inch skillet to ¾-inch depth. Heat oil to 375°F. Transfer frozen dough to hot oil with large spatula. Fry 4 or 5 cookies at a time until deep golden brown, 3 to 4 minutes, turning once. Remove cookies with spatula to paper towels; drain.

Combine remaining 4 tablespoons sugar with cinnamon. Place in paper bag. Add warm cookies 1 at a time; close bag and shake until cookie is coated with sugar mixture. Repeat with remaining sugar mixture and cookies. Remove cookies to wire racks; cool completely. Store tightly covered at room temperature or freeze up to 3 months.

*Makes about 3 dozen cookies*

**Spanish Churros**

# Crispy Duck

1 whole duck (about 5 pounds)
1 tablespoon dried rubbed sage
1 teaspoon salt
¼ teaspoon black pepper
3 cups vegetable oil
1 tablespoon butter or margarine
2 large Granny Smith or Rome Beauty apples,
    cored and cut into thin wedges
½ cup clover honey
   Fresh sage sprigs and crab apples for garnish

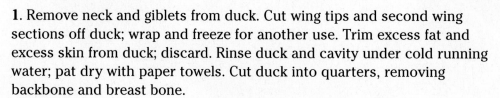

**1**. Remove neck and giblets from duck. Cut wing tips and second wing sections off duck; wrap and freeze for another use. Trim excess fat and excess skin from duck; discard. Rinse duck and cavity under cold running water; pat dry with paper towels. Cut duck into quarters, removing backbone and breast bone.

**2**. Place duck in 13×9-inch baking pan. Combine sage, salt and black pepper. Rub duck with sage mixture. Cover; refrigerate 1 hour.

**3**. To steam duck, place wire rack in wok. Add water to 1 inch below rack. (Water should not touch rack.) Cover wok; bring water to a boil over medium-high heat. Arrange duck, skin sides up, on wire rack. Cover; steam 40 minutes or until fork-tender. (Add boiling water to wok to keep water at same level.)

**4**. Transfer cooked duck to plate. Carefully remove rack from wok; discard water. Rinse wok and dry. Heat oil in wok over medium-high heat until oil registers 375°F on deep-fry thermometer. Add ½ of duck, skin sides down. Fry 5 to 10 minutes or until crisp and golden brown, turning once. Drain duck on paper towels. Repeat with remaining duck, reheating oil.

**5**. Pour off oil. Melt butter in wok over medium heat. Add apples; cook and stir 5 minutes or until wilted. Stir in honey and bring to a boil. Transfer apples with slotted spoon to warm serving platter. Arrange duck on apples. Drizzle honey mixture over duck. Garnish, if desired.   ***Makes 4 servings***

**Crispy Duck**

# Spicy Beef Tacos

1 pound boneless beef chuck, cut into 1-inch cubes
    Vegetable oil
1 to 2 teaspoons chili powder
1 clove garlic, minced
½ teaspoon salt
½ teaspoon ground cumin
1 can (14½ ounces) whole peeled tomatoes,
    undrained, chopped
12 corn tortillas (6-inch diameter)*
1 cup (4 ounces) shredded mild Cheddar cheese
2 to 3 cups shredded iceberg lettuce
1 large fresh tomato, seeded, chopped
    Cilantro for garnish

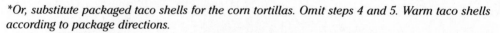

*Or, substitute packaged taco shells for the corn tortillas. Omit steps 4 and 5. Warm taco shells according to package directions.*

**1.** Brown beef in 2 tablespoons hot oil in large skillet over medium-high heat 10 to 12 minutes, turning frequently. Reduce heat to low. Stir in chili powder, garlic, salt and cumin. Cook and stir 30 seconds.

**2.** Add undrained tomatoes. Bring to a boil over high heat. Reduce heat to low. Cover and simmer 1½ to 2 hours until beef is very tender.

**3.** Using 2 forks, pull beef into coarse shreds in skillet. Increase heat to medium. Cook, uncovered, 10 to 15 minutes until most of liquid has evaporated and beef is moistly coated with sauce. Keep warm.

**4.** Heat 4 to 5 inches of oil in deep fat fryer or deep saucepan over medium-high heat to 375°F; adjust heat to maintain temperature.

**5.** For taco shells, place 1 tortilla in taco fryer basket;** close gently. Fry tortilla 30 seconds to 1 minute until crisp and golden. Open basket; gently remove taco shell. Drain on paper towels. Repeat with remaining tortillas.

**6.** Layer beef, cheese, lettuce and tomato in each taco shell. Garnish, if desired.
                                                          ***Makes 6 servings***

**Taco fryer baskets are available in large supermarkets and in housewares stores.*

**Spicy Beef Tacos**

# Chilaquiles

Vegetable oil
12 corn tortillas, cut into 1-inch strips
1 cup (1 small) chopped onion
1¾ cups (16-ounce jar) ORTEGA® Garden Style Salsa, medium or mild
1 cup (8-ounce can) CONTADINA® Tomato Sauce
2 teaspoons chili powder
½ teaspoon ground cumin
2 cups (8 ounces) shredded Monterey Jack or Cheddar cheese
¼ cup ORTEGA® Sliced Jalapeños
Sour cream (optional)
Sliced avocado (optional)

ADD oil to 1-inch depth in medium skillet; heat over high heat for 1 minute. Place tortilla strips in oil; fry, turning frequently with tongs, until light golden brown. Remove from skillet; place on paper towels.

POUR off all but 1 tablespoon oil from skillet. Add onion; cook for 1 to 2 minutes or until tender. Stir in salsa, tomato sauce, chili powder and cumin. Bring to a boil. Reduce heat to low; cook, stirring frequently, for 5 to 6 minutes.

LAYER half of tortilla strips in ungreased 13×9-inch baking pan. Top with half of sauce and half of cheese. Repeat layers. Bake in preheated 350°F. oven for 10 to 15 minutes or until cheese is melted. Top with jalapeños, sour cream and avocado just before serving.     ***Makes 8 servings***

**Tip:** Serve this traditional Mexican dish for breakfast, lunch or as an appetizer. Be creative and top with guacamole, sliced olives, chopped fresh tomatoes and, of course, additional ORTEGA® Sliced Jalapeños.

# Grandma's Apple Fritters

CRISCO® Oil for deep frying
1 egg, slightly beaten
½ cup milk
1 tablespoon CRISCO® Oil*
1 cup diced peeled apples or drained crushed pineapple
1 cup all-purpose flour
1 tablespoon granulated sugar
1 teaspoon baking powder
¼ teaspoon salt
1 cup confectioners' sugar
1 teaspoon ground cinnamon

*Use your favorite Crisco Oil product.

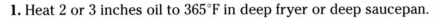

1. Heat 2 or 3 inches oil to 365°F in deep fryer or deep saucepan.

2. Combine egg and milk in large bowl. Stir in one tablespoon oil and apples or pineapple.

3. Combine flour, granulated sugar, baking powder and salt. Add to egg mixture. Stir just until mixed.

4. Drop by tablespoonfuls, a few at a time, into hot oil. Fry about 4 minutes or until golden brown. Turn as needed for even browning. Remove with slotted metal spoon. Drain on paper towels.

5. Combine confectioners' sugar and cinnamon in small bowl. Roll fritters in mixture. Serve warm.     ***Makes 6 to 8 servings***

## HOT HINTS

*To minimize spattering, never fill a skillet, deep fryer or saucepan more than half full of oil.*

# Mexican Fritters

1 cup water
½ cup butter or margarine
⅓ cup plus 1 teaspoon sugar, divided
¼ teaspoon salt
¼ teaspoon ground nutmeg
1 cup all-purpose flour
4 eggs
½ teaspoon vanilla extract
  Vegetable oil

**1.** Combine water, butter, 1 teaspoon sugar, salt and nutmeg in 2-quart saucepan. Heat over medium-high heat until butter is melted, stirring occasionally. Increase heat to high. Bring to a full rolling boil.

**2.** Add flour all at once to saucepan; remove from heat. Beat with wooden spoon until mixture forms smooth, thick paste. Cook and stir over medium-high heat 1 to 2 minutes until mixture pulls away from side of pan and forms a ball and a film forms on bottom of pan.

**3.** Add eggs, 1 at a time, beating vigorously after each addition until dough is smooth and shiny. Stir in vanilla. Let dough stand at room temperature 15 minutes.

**4.** Heat 1 inch oil in deep, heavy, large skillet over medium-high heat to 375°F; adjust heat to maintain temperature. Line baking sheet with paper towels.

**5.** Spoon dough into pastry bag or cookie press fitted with large star tip (about ½ inch).

**6.** Carefully press dough directly into hot oil in 6-inch-long strips, cutting strips with scissors to detach. Fry strips, 3 or 4 at a time, 5 to 7 minutes until brown, turning once. Gently remove with tongs or slotted spoon; drain well on paper towels. Repeat until all dough has been fried.

**7.** Roll warm strips in remaining ⅓ cup sugar to coat lightly.

*Makes about 18 strips*

Mexican Fritters

# Green's® "Dare to Dip 'em" Donuts

¼ cup (½ stick) butter, softened
⅓ cup granulated sugar
1 large egg
½ teaspoon vanilla extract
1¾ cups all-purpose flour, divided
1 teaspoon baking powder
1 teaspoon ground cinnamon
½ teaspoon baking soda
¼ teaspoon salt
⅓ cup buttermilk
Vegetable oil for frying
2 tablespoons powdered sugar
Chocolate Glaze (recipe follows)
½ cup "M&M's"® Chocolate Mini Baking Bits

In large bowl cream butter and granulated sugar until light and fluffy; beat in egg and vanilla. In medium bowl combine flour, baking powder, cinnamon, baking soda and salt. Alternately add one-third flour mixture and half of buttermilk to creamed mixture, ending with flour mixture. Wrap and refrigerate dough 2 to 3 hours. On lightly floured surface roll dough to ½-inch thickness. Cut into rings using 2½-inch cookie cutter; reserve donut holes. Heat about 2 inches oil to 375°F in deep-fat fryer or deep saucepan. Fry donuts, 2 to 3 at a time, about 30 seconds on each side or until golden brown. Fry donut holes 10 to 15 seconds per side or until golden brown. Remove from oil; drain on paper towels. Cool completely. Place donut holes and powdered sugar in large plastic food storage bag; seal bag. Shake bag until donut holes are evenly coated. Prepare Chocolate Glaze. Dip donuts into glaze; decorate with "M&M's"® Chocolate Mini Baking Bits. Store in tightly covered container. ***Makes 12 donuts and 12 donut holes***

## Chocolate Glaze

1 cup powdered sugar
1 tablespoon plus 1 teaspoon unsweetened cocoa powder
1 tablespoon plus 1 teaspoon water
¾ teaspoon vanilla extract

In medium bowl combine powdered sugar and cocoa powder. Stir in water and vanilla; mix well.

Green's® "Dare to Dip 'em" Donut

# Fried Norwegian Cookies
## (Fattigmandbakkelse)

2 large eggs, at room temperature
3 tablespoons granulated sugar
¼ cup butter, melted
2 tablespoons milk
1 teaspoon vanilla
1¾ to 2 cups all-purpose flour
    Vegetable oil
    Powdered sugar

Beat eggs and sugar in large bowl with electric mixer at medium speed until thick and lemon colored. Beat in butter, milk and vanilla until well blended. Gradually add 1½ cups flour. Beat at low speed until well blended. Stir in enough remaining flour with spoon to form soft dough. Divide dough into 4 portions; cover and refrigerate until firm, at least 2 hours or overnight.

Working with floured hands, shape 1 portion dough at a time piece into 1-inch-thick square. Place dough on lightly floured surface. Roll out dough to 11-inch square. Cut dough into 1¼-inch strips; cut strips diagonally at 2-inch intervals. Cut 1¼-inch slit vertically down center of each strip. Insert one end of strip through cut to form twist; repeat with each strip. Repeat with remaining dough portions.

Heat oil in large saucepan to 365°F. Place 12 cookies at a time in hot oil. Fry about 1½ minutes or until golden brown, turning cookies once with slotted spoon. Drain on paper towels. Dust cookies with powdered sugar. Cookies are best if served immediately, but can be stored in airtight container for up to 1 day.

***Makes about 11 dozen cookies***

**The publisher would like to thank the companies and organizations listed below for the use of their recipes and photographs in this publication.**

Bob Evans®

Chef Paul Prudhomme's Magic Seasoning Blends®

Colorado Potato Administrative Committee

ConAgra Grocery Products Company

Cucina Classica Italiana, Inc.

Filippo Berio® Olive Oil

Florida Department of Agriculture and Consumer Services, Bureau of Seafood and Aquaculture

The HV Company

Kikkoman International Inc.

Lawry's® Foods, Inc.

©Mars, Inc. 2001

McIlhenny Company (TABASCO® brand Pepper Sauce)

National Chicken Council

National Onion Association

Nestlé USA, Inc.

The Procter & Gamble Company

Reckitt Benckiser

USA Rice Federation

# METRIC CONVERSION CHART

## VOLUME MEASUREMENTS (dry)

1/8 teaspoon = 0.5 mL
1/4 teaspoon = 1 mL
1/2 teaspoon = 2 mL
3/4 teaspoon = 4 mL
1 teaspoon = 5 mL
1 tablespoon = 15 mL
2 tablespoons = 30 mL
1/4 cup = 60 mL
1/3 cup = 75 mL
1/2 cup = 125 mL
2/3 cup = 150 mL
3/4 cup = 175 mL
1 cup = 250 mL
2 cups = 1 pint = 500 mL
3 cups = 750 mL
4 cups = 1 quart = 1 L

## VOLUME MEASUREMENTS (fluid)

1 fluid ounce (2 tablespoons) = 30 mL
4 fluid ounces (1/2 cup) = 125 mL
8 fluid ounces (1 cup) = 250 mL
12 fluid ounces (1 1/2 cups) = 375 mL
16 fluid ounces (2 cups) = 500 mL

## WEIGHTS (mass)

1/2 ounce = 15 g
1 ounce = 30 g
3 ounces = 90 g
4 ounces = 120 g
8 ounces = 225 g
10 ounces = 285 g
12 ounces = 360 g
16 ounces = 1 pound = 450 g

## DIMENSIONS

1/16 inch = 2 mm
1/8 inch = 3 mm
1/4 inch = 6 mm
1/2 inch = 1.5 cm
3/4 inch = 2 cm
1 inch = 2.5 cm

## OVEN TEMPERATURES

250°F = 120°C
275°F = 140°C
300°F = 150°C
325°F = 160°C
350°F = 180°C
375°F = 190°C
400°F = 200°C
425°F = 220°C
450°F = 230°C

## BAKING PAN SIZES

| Utensil | Size in Inches/Quarts | Metric Volume | Size in Centimeters |
|---|---|---|---|
| Baking or Cake Pan (square or rectangular) | 8 × 8 × 2 | 2 L | 20 × 20 × 5 |
| | 9 × 9 × 2 | 2.5 L | 23 × 23 × 5 |
| | 12 × 8 × 2 | 3 L | 30 × 20 × 5 |
| | 13 × 9 × 2 | 3.5 L | 33 × 23 × 5 |
| Loaf Pan | 8 × 4 × 3 | 1.5 L | 20 × 10 × 7 |
| | 9 × 5 × 3 | 2 L | 23 × 13 × 7 |
| Round Layer Cake Pan | 8 × 1 1/2 | 1.2 L | 20 × 4 |
| | 9 × 1 1/2 | 1.5 L | 23 × 4 |
| Pie Plate | 8 × 1 1/4 | 750 mL | 20 × 3 |
| | 9 × 1 1/4 | 1 L | 23 × 3 |
| Baking Dish or Casserole | 1 quart | 1 L | — |
| | 1 1/2 quart | 1.5 L | — |
| | 2 quart | 2 L | — |